PILGRIMAGE TO NOWHERE

A Journey to Spiritual Enlightenment

Cover design by Gustav Davies

Library of Congress Control Number: 2025903660

ISBN: 979-8-9927189-0-4 (hardcover)

ISBN: 979-8-9927189-1-1 (paperback)

ISBN: 979-8-9927189-2-8 (e-book)

INTRODUCTION

For most of my life, I had the tendency to resist the middle ground. Usually, I was at zero or a hundred. I was either fully in or completely out. Against this background of "all or nothing" pattern of behavior, I was also very disciplined with a strict adherence to that discipline.

At school, I was a book worm. At work, I threw myself in. When I picked up an exercise routine, it was either do or die. When I drank, I drank a lot. I had once decided to smoke only one cigarette a day, after work, before bed. And for many, many years, I did exactly that.

If I was forced to compromise or succumb to the middle ground, my proclivity for escapism was particularly fierce. In order words, if things weren't going my way, then I was distraught. When I was distraught, life was tough and unmanageable. When life became unmanageable, I preferred drinking and smoking as a means of escape. That way, I didn't have to be particularly conscious of any experiences that were not to my liking.

Of course, I am only able to articulate this behavioral pattern in hindsight. And, the only relevance of this much introductory detail is solely to say that, this path of resistance via extremes and attachment to substances, with all its detriment to my body and mind and wellbeing, was, in the end, my path to Truth. How could it not?

PRELUDE

My first glimpse of Truth was in November 2019.

In the few years prior to 2019, the feeling of being trapped, bound by my own denseness, became unbearable. I sought many means of escape. I read spiritual books, attended AA meetings, completed a Kundalini Yoga Teacher's Training Program, taught yoga and meditation for a couple of years, and ventured into sound healing and alchemy. No matter which routes I embarked on, no matter where I turned, it seemed as if I traveled in a circle, always returning to the same place – my cage; that invisible grid that I had so efficiently built to separate and protect myself.

I had hopelessly hit my head against the wall of that cage many times but, on that day in November, by pure chance, or was it grace, there was a crack on the wall. A very tiny crack; just a narrow opening, really. But it was sufficient for me to gape at the unimaginable Truth beyond.

I needed to see more; to know more. There was an unretractable pull forward, an urge to traverse that barrier. There was no going back. And there were times, in the years that followed, when my yearning for Truth was frustrated, when I desperately wished to unsee and un-experience that moment. But I could not go back. I scurried around to find answers to my questions. But, at the time, I had to rely almost exclusively on YouTube videos as a primary source for research. You see, the world was gearing up to shut down due to Covid-19.

For the subsequent two years following that opening, I devoured video after video, searching, and desiring to know, and searching all over again and even deeper. It was amid this endless seeking that journaling emerged as a tool; a medium, if you will, for my mind to gather, condense, distill, and then formulate some logical framework of what I thought would lead to a conclusive insight of my experience. In hindsight, that initial foray into the nature of my existence was only a beginning.

Consequently, most of the journal entries are "questioning" by their very nature. Some are in the form of narratives, others as quasi-poetry. They are a running inventory of some of my most bizarre experiences and the inquiries that my mind had conjured up at the time. The questions evoked more questions and, at best, fleeting insights. Even the insights managed to evoke more questions and, hence, additional journal entries. A continuous process of evolving—a natural design by Grace.

These entries are in chronological order. Perhaps they might serve as a testament to the source of their truth.

AWAKENING — AN OPENING

I had taken a break from drinking. In its place, I picked up playing Candy Crush on my cell phone. When I arrive home from work, it was my escape from the thought and impulse to drink. And, true to character, I was obsessed with reaching the highest level as quickly as possible.

A peculiar thing happened yesterday.

I returned home from work and, my cell phone, which was fully charged minutes before I left work, was suddenly on low, red-alert, battery. All day yesterday, it showed signs of aging, blacking out and needing a complete shut-down and a turn-on again.

This was not the odd part. I'll get to that in a moment.

To avoid the risk of losing stored content on my phone, particularly, my saved Candy Crush current level, I immediately plugged in my phone to recharge and to initiate a back-up of its data to the laptop and an external drive.

Now, for the peculiar part: I had no contingency plans.

I'd backed up my cell phone data on numerous occasions in the past. I was familiar with the process and knew it could take upwards of thirty minutes. I was always prepared as to how to spend those thirty or so minutes. A glass of wine and a cigarette or two, if necessary, was sufficient to pass the time.

This time, there was clearly a predicament. I had decided not to drink for a few months so, in my mind, I could not drink. I also could not navigate away from the "backing up" screen on my phone. So, Candy Crush, my substitute lifeline, was inaccessible. I was at a loss on what to do. I smoked a cigarette. Cigarettes irritated my nerves, I knew that. But this time, restless agitation accompanied the nervous energy. Agitation turned to frustration and then a tantrum. A mind-body tantrum so visceral with heart palpitation and twitching of the body that I had to sit down in a self-embrace to still my body.

Out from nowhere, a thought arose, an echo from an Inner Engineering yoga course I had taken the previous week. It was a realization of sorts, "There is nothing I can do to change this moment, might as well accept it."

Something unfathomable happens at this juncture.

The sense of me and the sense of my body were no more. It completely vanished in an upward and outward rush. In its place, an Opening emerged. I was "in" the Opening but I was also "the" Opening. In the Opening, there was a "Ground" so deep and yet without depth or any dimensions at all. The Ground was at a distance infinitely beyond my reach. And yet, I was also the Ground.

I don't know how long this "experience" lasted.

Maybe for a few minutes? Most likely less than a minute. The shutter slammed shut and it disappeared as rapidly as it had appeared – as soon as my mind tried to understand what had just happened. But one impression remained with me: Whatever I do or do not do and whatever I think or do not think is undoubtedly happening in an Opening, within a Ground, all at once! And it seems that my body is also merely happening in it as well.

I was elated! "I am enlightened!", I thought.

Then questions followed in rapid succession, "So, what exactly am I, then"? "Where is this 'Opening' anyway"? "How is it possible for everything to happen all at once"?

I had no answers and no clue on how to obtain answers.

Frustration!

At the end of the day, what can I really say happened yesterday?

Frustration, Anger, Tantrum, A Breakthrough, An Opening, Many Questions, and back to Frustration.

All within the space of a few minutes.

DOUBT

Am I really that?

Whatever "that" is

Eerily, it seems to be present now

It seems to know

It seems to be aware

To be experiencing

My body & mind

Outside and inside

And everything between

All at once.

Really?

Infinite Surround Sound

Startled awake at 2:12am

New neighbor upstairs loves loud music

An extended new year's celebration, perhaps

This time, I went upstairs

To have an amicable chat—be a good neighbor

I knocked and knocked and knocked

No one came to the door

Perhaps, the music was too loud for him to
hear me

Perhaps not

I returned to my apartment and had a cigarette

An hour later, the music was still in full blast

And I could not fall back asleep

My mind, as it frequently does recently, drifted
to inquiry

What is the connection?

Between what I am

And my experience on November 11th?

How do "I" relate to "all at once?"

I've often heard the expression "Now" and
"Here"

Is "all at once" related to "Now" and "Here?"

What is this "Now"? Where is this "Here"?

In a flash, my thoughts, or rather, the movement
and sound of my thoughts, merged with the sound
of the music. And the objects in the room – my
bed, the nightstand, the desk, the ceiling fan, and
the bedroom walls – all appeared to be "happening" in the same space as my thoughts and the
music.

I, the sense of me, was the sounds and everything else

But I was nothing in particular

And I was here, in the same space

But I was nowhere in particular

It seemed as if I was everywhere

I was IT and I was ALIVE

Is this it, then?

Or has the journey just begun?

TIME

It's 5am

I feel nothing

But it is my meditation hour

That time count...

The focus on goals and objectives

It keeps me rooted in the body

And in my mind

When all I desire

Is to see and feel beyond it

A KNOWING FEELING

Sleep has become a rare commodity

Falling asleep is now

A practical exercise in wakefulness

Last night, I lay in bed

Silently waiting to fall asleep

A vague feeling arose

The sounds of my neighbor's footsteps upstairs

The occasional rumble of a car driving by

The ticking of the clock in the living room

The sound of my breadth

The slow and gentle rise & fall of my chest

They were all arising from me and known by me

It was just a feeling

Accompanied by knowing

A type of knowing

That was beyond intellectual understanding

It was not at all a pervasive feeling

But it was there for a moment

PASSING

KB passed away today

An entire city mourns

A lifetime of accomplishments

Now relegated

As a matter for history

I am compelled to think about others

My favorite composers

Whose music infuse aliveness

The magnitude of their gifts to humanity

They are not aware

The value of their music today

They cannot know

How I cherish their gift of music

I am overwhelmed by sadness

We live only for a short time

So, I ask

What does one do with a brief life?

What does it mean to be alive?

And if I were to live for a thousand years

Is my experience "right now" not all that counts?

Is it not all there is?

Is living fully for one moment

Not worth more than a thousand lifetimes

Of mediocrity?

Of ceaseless toil and expectations?

ANIMATED EARTH

Last night in meditation

The experience of my body

Was very distinct

My body was pulsating

And weightless

It was empty

And pure

It was animated

Condensed vibrations

Localized on earth

BODY

Experientially right now

This is the sense of my body:

Sparkles

Tingling Vibrations

Unending Movement

A Dance

Suspended in Space

But which one am I?

Where am I?

My mind feels entitled

To formulate a definition

I am desperately attempting

To latch onto something

Disorientation

Am I

That pulsating, vibrating wave?

The Pok-a-dots

Appearing and disappearing?

Ungraspable

In motion, constant motion

If I am that

Then who is it?

Or what is it?

That is actually experiencing me

That is constantly knowing me

As me

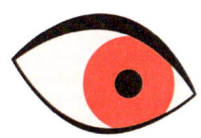

Spirit at the Foreground

Unwavering

Assertive

Awake and present

As my first love

My first love; My last love

My in-between love

A love that shines

By it. Through it. As it

It not being

Yet Being as complete

A vessel

Void

Yet full of grace

Clear, without texture

Yet, magnetic and demure

Embracing

Claiming and Allowing

Assertively allowing

A joyous reminder of aliveness

THOUGHT (A MEDITATION)

I am aware

A non-linear, formless movement

A vibrating wave of motion

Arising from me; as myself

I am aware

Dissipating into me; as myself

I am aware

Experiencing; Knowing

I am aware

A Realization

I am pure movement

I am not separate from my movements

All movements are made of me

As me

In me

And by me

Only me

I imbue my movements with experience

I appear as myself

This much I understand

My Guru

Two weeks ago, during morning meditation, a small lizard suddenly appeared, lazing nonchalantly on my yoga mat. I don't know how it entered my bedroom. I can't explain from where it came. But it was the second of such appearing and disappearing incidents in my bedroom. The first was eighteen months earlier. A crystal bowl slipped from my hand, fell to the floor, and disappeared.

So, last night, there I was in the middle of a Rupert Spira's Yoga Meditation titled, "You are the only substance present in your experience."

Angry. No, I was actually fuming because…

Well, because I had been cornered.

I wanted a drink. My mind conjured up all the usual reasons why it was alright to drink. But I could not drink. I was afraid.

That Lizard was a Guru. It shone a mirror on my state of mind.

Or rather, it showed very clearly where I was not.

I was not afraid of the lizard. As a child, I grew up with different species of lizards darting around in the courtyard. But I was terrified of what else might show up. If I don't let go of my attachment to escapism, what will my Guru appear as the next time?

Curiously, as I sat down to meditate this morning, there was a shift of energy from "fear" to "re-examination."

"Who was it that was upset, so afraid and angry last night"?

"What is it that fiercely resists, determined to hold on to the status quo"?

"Why is there such an immense compulsion to have things my way"?

I can't find the "who" or "what." And I don't know the "why." But I'm hopeful. One of these days, perhaps like the lizard, it will reveal itself or, at least, disclose where the crystal bowl is hiding so I can take a closer look.

INVENTORY

Having experientially explored my body & mind for the past few months, what do I really know to be true?

- I am aware
- My body is an amalgamation of shapeless sensations
- My thoughts are vibrations
- My perceptions are also vibrations

What else do I "sort-of" know?

- My body & mind are appearances
- They are like "activities" and "happenings"
- They are happening "here" all at once
- "Here" feels like an open space.

There's a gap. It feels as if something is missing.

- My body continues to be my reference point as "I"
- Experience is still separated into subject/object pools
- And somewhere at the back of my mind, a formulated but unspoken agenda chirps away…
- ✓ Dissolve the subject/object experience!
- ✓ Merge experience into one!

CRYING

I am in bondage

Reluctantly, I admit

And I hold on

A willing prisoner of attachments

Food, Caffeine, Nicotine

I taste with one hand; inhale with the other

A dawning of my imprisonment

Sadness

By grace

Simple, familiar, yet unmistakable grace

Some attachments have been vanquished

For others, I hold on

Ignorance

I weep

I am beat

I weep with realization

But I cling to the illusion

With hope

I inhale again

The sweet fragrance of surrender

A good distance away

I wait

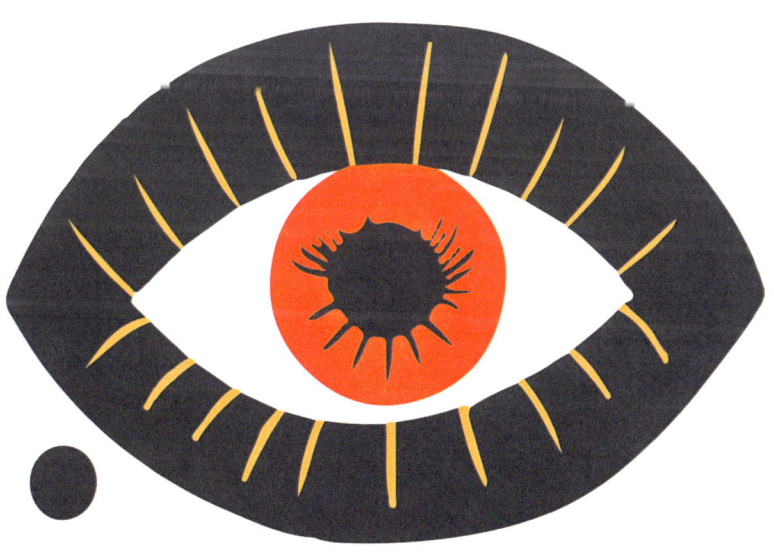

CELEBRATION

Something is happening

Celebrate something

Life is happening

Celebrate life

I am happening

Celebrate I am

Mysterious

I am a mystery

From where do my thoughts arise?

Where do they reside?

I close my eyes

All I find are tingles and dots

Vibrations and waves

Nothing but movement

Flowing nothingness

Unto itself

Confusion reigns

Which am 1?

What am I?

Which am I not?

Genuinely, I do not know

MY GOD

My God is everywhere

I reach out and touch

But he is nowhere

He just flows and floats

He peers through my eyes and sees himself in me, as him

He knows me in himself, as himself, made of himself, by himself

At times my God feels distant

But at this moment, I know

He is here

Everywhere

Nowhere

Now!

Edges

Two ends of a pillow…

The edges of a table….

Square points of a screen…

The points of an angle…

Platforms…

The beginning and the end of an alphabet…

The end of a circle…

I am surrounded…

So much impermanence…

Non-Engagement

Allowing the mind

To do what it is designed to do

And it is well designed

Its performance exceeds expectations

But there's no need to be unsettled

No need to be annoyed

No need to be irritated

About thinking

Don't fuss over it

Don't engage it

Allowing thinking to be

Fear

I am afraid to express

I am afraid to be

I am afraid of being afraid

I am fully locked-in

Not truly

An authentic expression

Of whatever it is that I am

The fear of fear has become

A solid roadblock

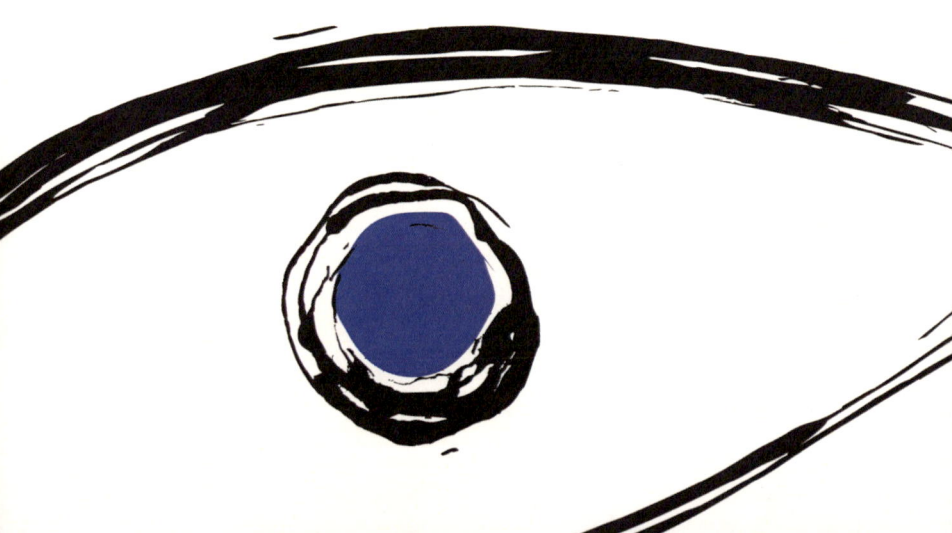

PREFERENCES

What is the nature of preferences?

The preferences for people

The preferences for things

The preferences for places

What are its attributes?

Here, I am guarded

In Europe, I come alive

In Italy, I live fully

What does it have to do with what I am?

Why does it matter?

Does it matter?

What's Next?

This ailment persists

It appears in varied forms

Sometimes well dressed and masked

As ambition and motivation

Other times, it shows up in drags

As restlessness

In all its forms

Highbrow or downtrodden

There's an unequivocal presence of dissatisfaction

There's a need for "that next thing"

The next minute, hour, day

The next week. A five-year plan?

Without which a cloud of sadness engulfs

The clarity to see this much

Is surely an act of Grace

Now, for the courage?

The courage to allow

Courage to release the sadness

To empty out discomfort from the "What's Next"

Courage to welcome

The space of Being

ANOTHER MOMENT

Last November, I understood that whatever I was, I was "happening" in an eternal space. Over the course of several months, I've also realized that the body, which I previously referred to as "I" was merely an unstructured vibration; an activity within the same eternal space. For the last few weeks, I've felt time merging. Weeks, days, and hours seem to be collapsing into moments. As if time is irrelevant. But these realizations, though experiential and genuine, fell short. They lacked the quality of completion.

This morning upon waking

I was living Eternity

It is ONE

It is NOW

Viscerally!

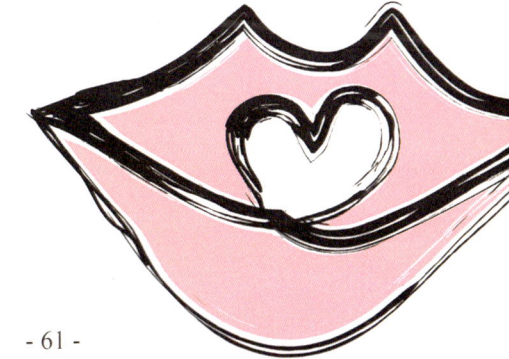

THOUGHT

Oh, what beauty!

The power of the mind

To remember

To imagine

To fantasize

Consciously

The paradox does not escape!

To allow it

Welcome it

With open arms

The release unto empty space

That is I

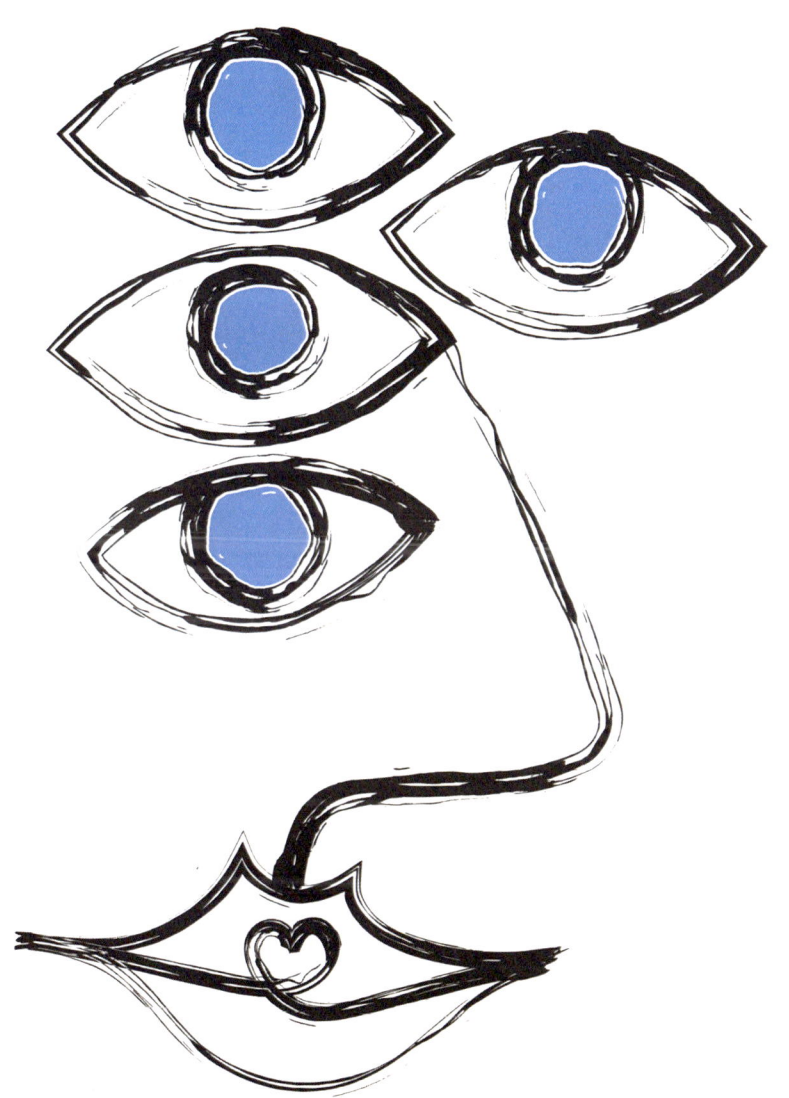

FLOW

A gravitational pull

An unequivocal preference

To remain with the open movement

The functional contractions of the body

Are reluctant to perform

Less they interfere with the flow

My body becomes

Subtler and lighter

It feels sweet, very sweet

Sweetness

The beauty of nonattachment

An Early Moring Thought

As thou

Hast let me come unto thee

My heart opens unto thee

LETTER TO ADYA

Dear Adya,

Thank you for teaching with love and compassion.

I am in limbo at the moment. I have zero orientation. What I've heard you describe in your teachings as the "orienting principle of the psychological self" has disappeared. When did it disappear? I do not know. I didn't know that it was there until it was no longer present and there's nothing left; nothing at all.

I keep asking myself, "What's next?" or to use your phrasing, "What's life calling forth in me?" I haven't a clue. So, I ask, "When and how does a new orienting principle begin to settle in the body, below the neck? Again, I don't know. In fact, the only thing I know right now with any semblance of certainty is that I DO NOT KNOW.

Of course, knowing that I don't know is somewhat liberating. Nevertheless, there remains a fair amount of restlessness and of general dissatisfaction. For someone like me, the queen of "to-do list," who had once placed so much emphasis on career achievements, this is a disconcerting place to be.

Your heart and open-mindedness practices from Sessions 1&2 and the pointers from Session 1 (i.e., it's not a matter of mind and that there is nowhere to go, but rather that it's a shift of reference out of the one that is trying to get there) have been most helpful. But, I keep getting caught. I just don't know how to let go. Sometimes, I think, "Oh, I get it. I understand what Adya means." But moments later, I realize that I don't know what you meant.

Invariably, I get caught up with the restlessness and I find something, anything to do. Some harmless; others not so much. I sense that at the end of the day, these activities, harmless or not, equate to the same thing: Escaping from the discomforts of a lack of orientation or motivation to do anything productive. Although, I can see this game of hide and seek clearly, I cannot find the courage to just sit with the discomfort and disorientation and allow everything to be as it is.

I wonder, please, would you mind providing additional pointers? Perhaps, particularly about things/practices one ought to refrain from doing, so as not to impede the process of awakening at the level of the heart?

Warm Regards

Afoma

****

Please find below my notes/jottings, written in
a moment of restlessness just before Session 3
began last night. I only include it here as a ded-
ication to you to say, "Thank you!" Thank you
for making your teachings so readily and widely
available to the general public. It has been a great
source of strength and direction for me over the
last two years.

I hope you'll receive it with your endearing openness.

Remembering – A Reminder

My body is quivering again

I close my eyes

Dotted Sparks

Vibrating, twisting and turning

An endless, amorphous dance

Encircling in constant movement

I long for wholeness

Then, I remind myself to remember

I am that in which the quivers happen

I am that before the quivers happen

I am the quivers

Silently, I indulge an invocation; a prayer of sorts

I pray to let "the mind" of the quivers to just be

I pray to know once more what I really am

Before the mind of separation usurped my domain

I pray to collapse "the mind" of the quivering body unto myself

I pray to reclaim the foreground of myself

To give myself to myself

EVERYDAY

An easy glide and navigation

As the witness

Thoughts, concepts, words, ideas

All appear in an illusory platform

My body as a constant, formless movement

Is slowly normalizing

Hearing happens in me

Though rarely as me

Objects are experienced

As appearing within me

These are new norms for perceiving

And sometimes

I am expanded enough

To catch a coup d'œil

Of oneness in visual perceptions

Autonomous & Unconstrained

Two Saturdays ago, I had a piano lesson at mid-day. I just could not play. Weeks of continuous, decreasing motivation to do anything seemed to have culminated during the lesson. My fingers would not move. Customary bodily contractions were tense and rigid. There was no life force in my body to engage any movement.

And yet

Sitting there

I was very aware

And equally mesmerized

By the halting of my body's movements

The lack of modulation of form

The grand takeaway?

My body is a crucial agent for experience

Consciousness unembodied

As was the case during my piano class

Is a cessation of expression in this body form

But

Consciousness is independent of my body

Absolutely, yes!

The lack of a body

The physical death of my body

Does not cancel consciousness

A Moment of Knowing

In meditation

Last Thursday, October 22nd

Rupert Spira's Yoga Meditation

"Emptiness Moving in Emptiness,"

One sentence

"See that the space is not a physical space. It is a knowing space…"

A portal of understanding opened

There and then

I understood

I could see it

I am ever-present

I am openness

All experiences happen within me

In my daily life since then

Without "formal" meditation

My body

My thoughts

And the 10,000 other things

Clearly appear in me

They are "happening" within me

Am I what I've been searching for?

BODY REVISITED

Eyes closed

I contemplate

The current experience of my body

Open

Vibrations

Sensing

Knowing

Knowing the sensing

Unlocated knowing

That's all

MIND REVISITED

How my mind loves to drift

Fancies and Fantasies

Recalls

Imaginations and Impressions

Far away

Always so very, very far away

Anywhere but here

Anytime but now

And yet

Anything and everything

That is real

Is nowhere but

Now and Here

MEMORY

In quiet sitting

Or during formal meditation

These things are obvious to me

The experience of my body

Is that of movement

Movement without a definite form

There are some clusters, yes

But even the clusters.

Are ever changing

Constantly in motion

An unending eternal dance

The image of my body

Is merely an imprint

A memory in my mind

An Owl in Eternity — A Reveal

I went to Café Commissary to lounge away my lunch hour. It was routine. Half a chocolate chip cookie and a cappuccino later, I gathered up my affairs and stepped outside to walk the short ten minutes home.

In an instant, without notice

I merged into the open space

All movements became lighter and brighter

I had a mild sense of having a body

But I had no head

Yes, a headless body

With only two eyes

That took interim occupancy of the headspace

Both eyes were big and wide and round

Like that of an owl

With 360 degrees of knowing

I could see that it was all me

I took a few steps forward

The pavement was me

I stood still and looked around

The road was me

The parking meters were me

The cars driving by were me

All the buildings were me

I looked up at the sky

And it was me

The vast openness

Was made of me

The entire landscape

Appeared in me

It was all myself

Minutes passed

Maybe only seconds passed

Again, in an instant

I was back

In my body & mind

As a solid self

Disappointed

I wanted it to last

Just a little longer

Completely enthralled

By the experience

A moment of Beauty

A tiny taste of Oneness

Unity at my doorstep

Beckoning

I was eager

To understand this life

The nature of my existence

REFERENCE POINT

Is the I

That I am

These body sensations?

The constant movements of waves

That I feel

Is that me?

I am searching for a reference point

An objective reference for my experience

There's an ongoing thug of war

Either contract into the body & mind

To objectively experience the movements

Or let go and surrender

To the knowing

I am sensing

That there is no point of reference

But I'm not deterred

From desiring it

From seeking it

Afterall

This is separation

Elsewhere

Sadness in the body

Aimless disenchantment

Run!

No, No, No!

The legs are tired

The back is grieving

So, I hop

Around and around

Away from the disquiet, I think

Soon thereafter

A contrasting movement arises

A dance takes shape

Amidst the sadness

Surrounded by disquiet

Happiness begins its invasion

In the background

There is peace

I am back home

Where I always was

EXPANSION

Sitting or standing

I feel and experience my body differently

The space behind my body

Often rigid

An impenetrable wall of resistance

Is unfolding

Yielding to a stronger force

The movement of my body

Is constant and consistent

The sensations and contractions

That I know as my body

Are being pulled apart

As if they are being dissolved

Into the Openness

Observations

My head feels empty

The vibration of thinking is palpable

I can almost see them

My heart opens to perceive

In these moments

Perhaps just for an instant

Thinking happens in an openness

Not in my head

And my body sensations

Do not need a reference point

It's purely "Sensing"

A Subtle Shift

Upon waking this morning

My body lay in bed

But the sense of I

Was far wider

Than the body in bed

Expanded

Without dimension

And

The sound of the truck on the street

Was not being perceived

Through my ears

Hearing was happening here

Along with seeing

An integral shift in perception

ANOTHER SHIFT

My field of energy

Is in slow transition

From terse and intense

To lighter and breezy

The extensive traction

Reinforced by the push-pull opposition

From my body's resistance_

Is weakening

Dissipating

An open field is taking up space

Inhabiting the foreground

My body sensations

Are happy to simply float

In the surrounding emptiness

Relegating aversion

To the back

Nonetheless

A sense of separation persist

My Heart

Sitting at my desk

I feel my heart flowing over

Standing by the piano

The piano and sheet music

Arise within me

During meditation

I see my heart pouring out

Expanding beyond

An infinite expansion

Into eternity

There is nothing but experience

LIMINAL SPACE

Continuous swaying

Movement of the body

Suspended in limbo

The impulse to reference the movement

Never fully resting in the midst of experience

Nor fully identified with the body

But resting as consciousness

In the midst of a chaotic day

Is also becoming customary

Today, it felt normal

There was no need to strain

No where to try to get to

Just Being

THE YOD

Here

There's transparency

Presence

Oneness of perception

No self

Oneness of Being

Nothing

No absence

Effortless

THE WAR AGAINST SURRENDER

How is it possible

That I have nothing to do

This is my mind's predominant narrative

I must be doing something

There must be something I should be doing

As if rephrasing the question

Validates the narrative

There are things I could do

I could watch a movie

Or read

Or write

Or learn a new language

Or compose music

Or play the piano

Perhaps a more intellectual or creative pursuit

Legitimizes the need to avoid being still

But there's no need for legitimacy

I have no motivation to do any of it

Nothing, at all, is of interest to me

Nothing, at all, is compelling enough to engage

Moreover, whatever I can summon up energy to do

Fills so little time

This realization generates waves

Discomfort and fear run down my spine

So, I eat something

And I smoke afterwards

That eases the immediate discomfort

Temporarily

The cycle of mind narrative begins again…

Inexplicable

I went to bed at 11:00 p.m. last night.

Woke up at 1:30 a.m.

My entire body was charged

With electrical impulses

Flowing currents

With high intensity in my legs and my feet

And around my chest

Not an unusual occurrence

For the past few months

This time

I placed my left hand and palm on my chest

To brace some of the intensity

Mystery

My hand and palm dissolve into my chest

My breath, chest, palm, hands were one movement

Without boundaries

And only one thought arose

Spirit awakening in the Body

As the Body

A Happy Place

To not resist the mind

To not engage the mind

To rest in this aliveness

As Eternal Presence

To know that I am

To be always available

Always in the background

Of all expressions

Of all experience

To be that

I AM

STUCKNESS

Reasons for discomfort are plentiful

Thoughts, sensations, feelings

Lack of engagement to

Play the piano

Compose music

Write

Learn a new language

Meditate

Inability to redirect

Stop smoking

Lose weight

Strengthen body

Sadness at every turn

Desiring

Unfulfillment of desires

Insufficiency of fulfilled desires

Aloneness

Freedom

Beautiful music

Sad music

Not Knowing

Causes for dis-ease are abound

These are agonizing times

Full Moon Flirtation

"Allow what is to be as it is"

I am familiar with that catchy phrase

Intellectually, I understand it

To allow is to be present

Today

At morning meditation

Allowing very quietly snuck in

An open corridor

For a passage to freedom

A deepening of Presence

I was happy for no reason

THE SWING

Back and forth

From oneness to separation

I've heard it described

As the swing of a pendulum

This feels more akin to

The motion of

A windshield wiper

On a day with light drizzle

There's a slow dial to the opposite direction

A wide arc between two extreme postures

An unnecessarily long pause at separation

This wide swing has changed

Its velocity has accelerated

Momentum rapid

Its arc has shortened

The two positions

Moving closer and closer together

The pause at separation wickedly reduced

A windshield wiper

On a day of heavy downpour

With urgency

To remove any precipitation

No. A great urgency

To blade away all debris

To enforce clarity

The result

A shortening in circuitry

A compressed and glitchy medium

An unstable field, at best

Impossible to energize

An unstable electromagnetic platform

Unfeasible to operate

Giving way to

Radical, unintended non-doing

A DYING DEATH

I am dying

It's a recurring thought

When I wake up in the morning

It's a feeling I cannot shake

All through the day

My body senses the same

It sends a clear message

As I lay down to sleep

I am dying

My Dearest

I remain the same for you

You who are a captive

Of time and its lines

You who are caught

In linearity

A timeline of myself within me

I embrace you with love

I hold you in my bosom

I am

DISCOMFORT

Discomfort from Aliveness

The emergence of aliveness

From its burrows

Buried deep

In the grave of ignorance

Discomfort from Choosing

The making of a choice

That avoids discomfort

In a moment

In anticipation of fear

Discomfort from a Choice

A contrary choice

That meets the fear

But it leaves room

For the experience of a subsequent fear

That itself

Is a source of irritation

Fear of Discomfort

The impulse to escape

My favorite escape route

Now ends at the fridge

A consolation prize

For having endured

One minute of fear

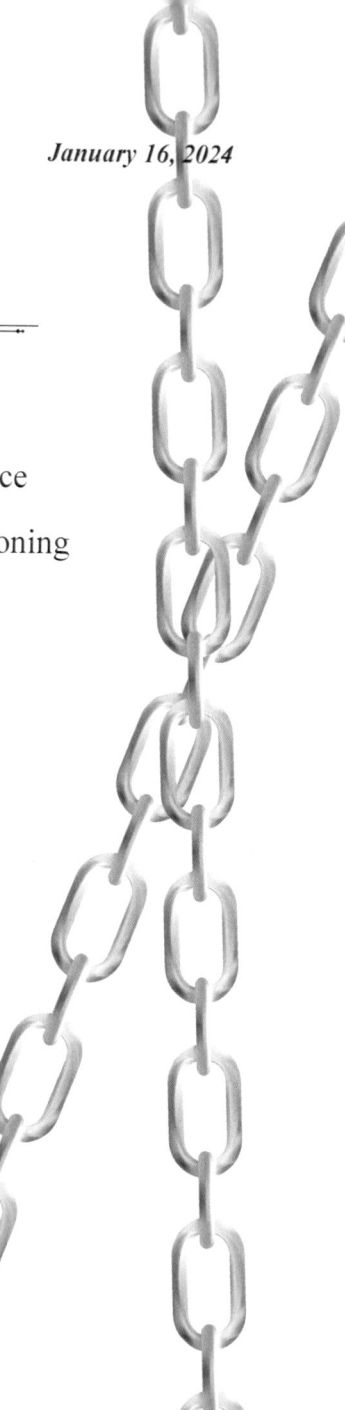

Slavery

Captivated by sense perceptions

Captured by the flow of experience

Disgruntled as a result of conditioning

But bound by the chain of events

Tilted by disequilibrium

Veiled from clarity

Enslaved by desires

Placated by meager alms

But perpetually seeking

Proclamations of freedom

I Slave for my mind

I Slave for my body

Hierarchy of Avoidance

Body Sensation

Discomfort

Devise a means of distraction

Avoid the discomfort by any means and at all costs

Fear of discomfort

Become smart about managing discomforts

Identify circumstances of discomfort

Anticipate and prepare ahead to avoid those instances

Fear of the Fear of discomfort

Choose only those actions

That enable avoidance of the fear of discomfort

Any choice, no matter how reasonable

That is contrary to the avoidance of the fear

Meet it with deep-seated dissent and angst

I am now further removed from the discomfort

So much further away from the dreaded *sensation*

It's become more about the fear

It's always been about the fear

How do I avoid being afraid of the fear?

ANTAGONIST

Any attempt

To allow and stay with discomfort

Serves as an invitation

The mind gears up

It heralds-in

In full antagonist mode

Noisy

Loud

It leaves no angle unturned

Calculating

Scheming

Conniving

Strategizing

That devious mastermind

Devises and presents to itself

The best feasible solution

Under the circumstances

Anything to remain relevant

Anything to be front and center

Any route to get back

In the driver's seat

To steer the wheels of separation

Dawn

My mind is at its playground

Intent on playing out diverse roles

Amidst the drama

Its six-member casting directors

Remain fully engaged

Pointing, Critiquing, Snickering

But never ever reaching a quorum

Just at the height of anticipation

As the curtain fall precedes Act 2

A flash of clarity emerges

A ray of light penetrates

My mind takes on a different role

Of one who is less lost in ignorance

Let the mind play or not play

It echoes

What's there to resist?

Who's there to resist except the mind?

A joyful encapsulation

Of its activities for the last fifteen minutes

I've become accustomed

To my mind's theatrics

A sense of well-being

Instills and situates

Amidst the noise

Deep in the recessed background

It is well

THINKING

Never-ending
Waves of movement
Characteristically discriminatory
Between This and That
Continuously divisive
Separating
That one from
This one from
The other

Waves of sadness flutter
Anxiety floats by on its tails
Quivers of nerves follow suit in pursuit
Hula hoops of twirling vibrations
Subsets of the One
As the One
Appearing and disappearing

CONSEQUENTIAL SURRENDER

Full of Disappointment

Replete with Sadness

Deplete of Aliveness

A remarkable inability

To direct life's energies

A strong presence

Of passion for life

With a competing

Low-density vitality

Desire and Drive

Deadness and Disinclination

All are of equal measure

Surrender is Victorious

As a Consequence

Dispersed Discomfort

This sense of discomfort

Has a different quality

It is inviting, whispering…

It's alright to explore

Understand the nature of discomfort

It's ok to linger

Massage the fabric of this discomfort

Intimately feel its texture

There is no need to run

There's nowhere to go

By Design

Thinking

Has no discipline

It does not discriminate

Amongst its many discriminations

It can have insights

In a blue moon

It is often surprised by

Its own capacity to imagine

Its own incapacity to fathom

By design

Thinking is miraculous

It is equally endearing

In The Body Again

I fall back asleep

Yet again

Identified with body sensations

Although the time

Between waking and sleeping

Merge closer and closer

Oscillating back and forth

Like one taking a catnap

Ready to blink away asleepness

By a gentle nudge

When I am in the body

Those moments when the mind

Seemingly overrides awareness

I am not completely asleep

Sensations are experienced

As mere appearances

To an "observer"

And moments of awakeness

Are fully charged with

Rich and electrifying aliveness

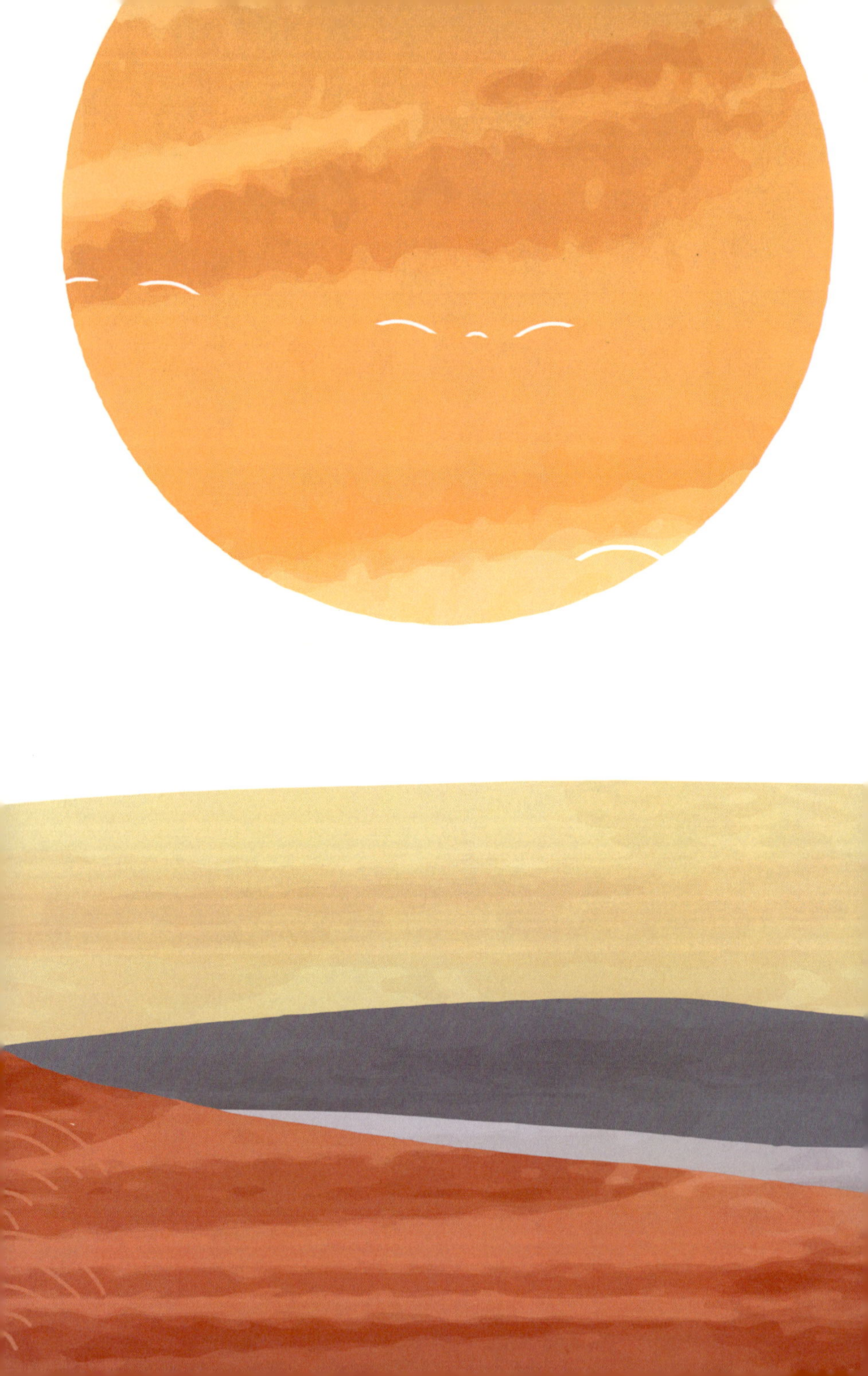

FLOATING

In the presence of Truth

Unidentified

Unconcerned

Without knowing

Without worry

In a void of completion

A void of potentiality

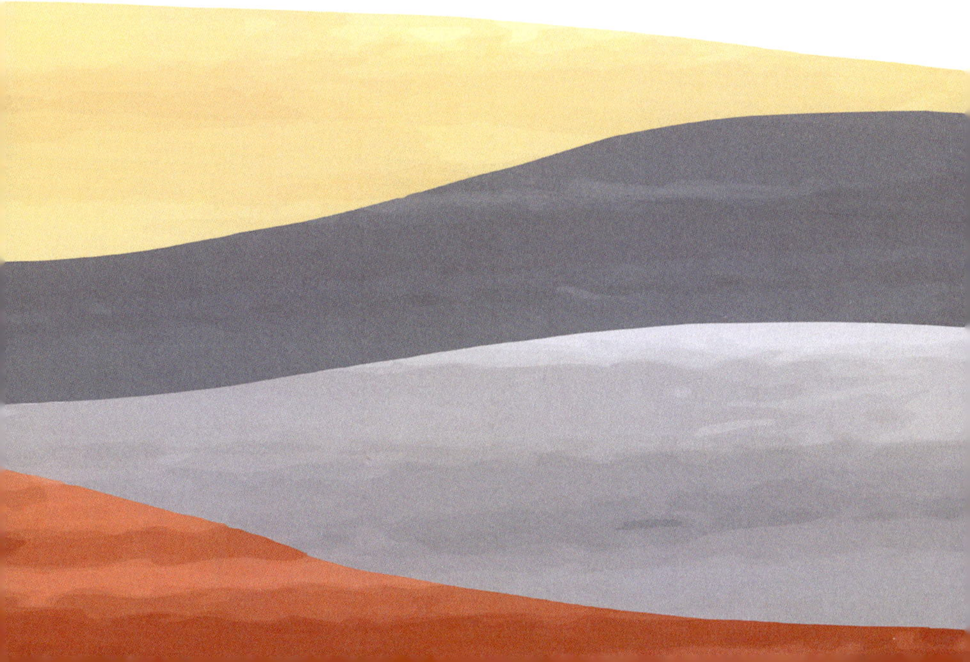

A Reminder

These configurations of thought

These silhouettes of body sensation

Are movements of myself

Appearances of myself in myself

This separate self

Ever disjointed and disparate

Finds them uncomfortable

These thoughts

These sensations

To assimilate them

Is to be free

Of their apparent discomforts

In union

Fully embodied as myself

Realization Disrupted

I can't think

No. I am thinking

Thinking is on full acceleration

Thoughts are fluttering by

No time to discern their gibberish

Sensations are equally undecisive

Whether to settle down

Or continue their rapid maneuvers

It's all moving so fast

Sensations

Thoughts

Feelings

Swirling on a collision course

Yet

There's stagnation

There's stuckness

There's helplessness

What to do?

Run or stay?

Which way to turn?

Where to go?

It is a multi-road intersection

Instinctively

I know they all lead to a dead end

Impulsively

I'm screaming

Find a shortcut!

But it's too noisy

Too loud

Too busy

And

I'm deplete of gimmicks

No new efficient tool within reach

The choice is simplified

Just hang in there

Do nothing!

Two Competing Discomforts

Temporary Discomfort

From fillers

Caffeine and Nicotine

Fillers used to avoid

The permanence of a void

An unavoidable, overshadowing void

Looming uncomfortably close

And drawing closer each moment

Fillers destabilize experience

Yet, their pull is over-reaching

Demanding

Tolerable

Because each time

With each indulgence

The discomforts pass

Albeit momentarily

An apparent preference

For the mind

An extraordinary exhibition

Of a high tolerance

For suffering

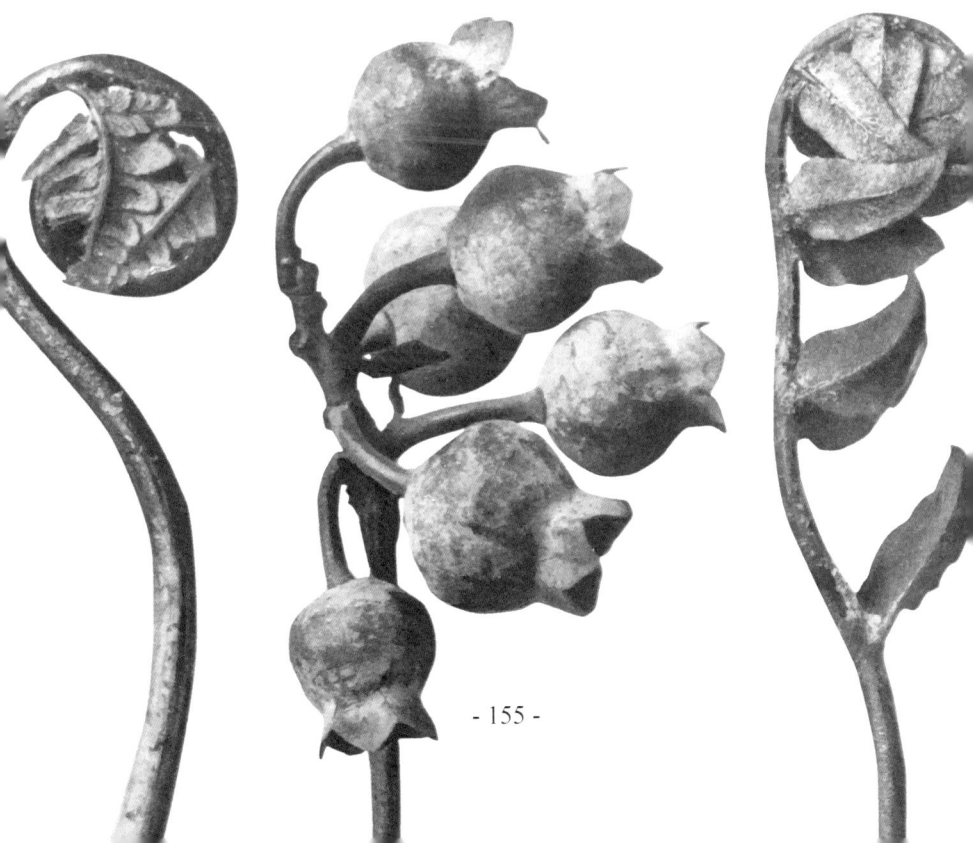

Two Competing Discomforts

Permanent Discomfort

Due to nothingness

A continuous grasping

Towards form

Something, anything

And finding

That there's nothing compelling

There is understanding

A realization of what is

But understanding no longer soothes

And realization does not alleviate

The lived experience of discomfort

Nor does it afford an escape

From the imperative:

Allow what is to be

So. it is very clear
The only way out
Is to dive in
Heart first
Without abandon

Empty Fillers

Eventually

Fillers betray themselves

As common enhancers

An extra dose to heighten

Useless gadgets to augment

Aimless ornamentation

They do nothing but prolong

The experience of discomfort

And only bursts of frustration remain

In their wake

What happens

When fillers are no longer filling?

When they are no longer satisfying?

When they are revealed to be mere fluff

As empty as the entirety of their ingredients

Ultimately

The entrapment exposes itself

Entrapment for a compromise

Entrapped

By the fear of emptiness

By the desire to escape the nothingness

By the promise of a better something

Release

Allowing discomfort

To permeate within

Pains my heart

A thick barrier of resistance

Against a robust and outward push

The aftermath?

A sharp release of something

Dare I say

Something stuck at the heart center

A release rarely sustained

But felt all the same

A tingling amazement

A lightness of the heart

A different, broader, wider, freer perspective

From within

Agility from Spirit by Spirit

Allowing…. Remembering….

Get closer and closer to the fear

Allowing… Remembering…

Two perspectives of the one equation

Nothing extra-ordinary

As long as I have a body&mind

There is Experience

But Consciousness is ON

No matter the condition of this body&mind

I am aware

No matter what I'm aware

Do I want to be completely lost in experience

Or

Would I prefer to consciously engage in experience

This, for me

Is the question of the day

It is not at all complicated

Nor is it extraordinary

Why did it take so long

For this realization to settle in?

Why has there been

So much resistance?

Along the way

What was there to it?

To engage or disengage

To entangle or disentangle

To be or not to be

A radical interpretation?

A Realized Perspective

I can engage in phenomenon
As I am
And to my heart's content
I dance with all of my allure
At illusions of myself
I bathe
In the miracle of my ordinariness
Unremarkably at peace
How fantastically delirious I get
With my distractions
Of pain and pleasure
I am amused
The intoxicating presence of beauty
Are forever displayed
Against a steadfast background
Of Peace and Happiness
Experience is magical!

YOGA

My body is dense

Deplete of energy

Exhausted

From constant and unnecessary tussle

Between an inherent push for expansion

And the apparent discomfort caused

By the imminent expansion

Exhausted

From my mind's captivity

By thoughts and feelings

In the face of discomfort

Such turbulence in energies

Energy spent on allowing

Making room for discomforts

My body remains the weak link

It cannot keep up

Full involvement a distant nemesis

What tiny quantities there are of its energies

Are reluctant to redirect

From meaningless charter and noise

Activities of the mundane

Towards any semblance of conscious action

Not even a compelling desire for creativity

Can entice it

Unable to sustain vibrations

Possessed and overcome by impulses

Propelled towards never-ending movement

Useless movement

Preferring hours of sitting

Hours of clicking through media

But I remain aware

Aware and perfectly independent

From the condition of this body

Aware of the paradox of being

And the desire to move

The desire to create

Through this body

This body

A tool for creation

Pervaded by conditioning

Riddled with dis-ease

Is not at its peak of health

So, I continue

On the path of Yoga

LAYERED CHORDS

This middle layer of connection

As an observer

It enjoys a level of solace

Comfortable as the witness

As an afterthought

It delights in corrections

And assigns itself

The cushy, arrogant job of negation

Negate a feeling

Rephrase a thought

Feel better, Sound better

A better perspective

An enlightened perspective

As if to say, "I see you, 'mind!'"

Don't be fooled!

Identity rogue

Is its ardent vocation

An ancient impostor

Usurper of reality

Its corrective movement

Serves only as self-reconstitution

An anchor in separation

A deeper attachment to an object

Albeit the subtle objects

Of thoughts and of feelings

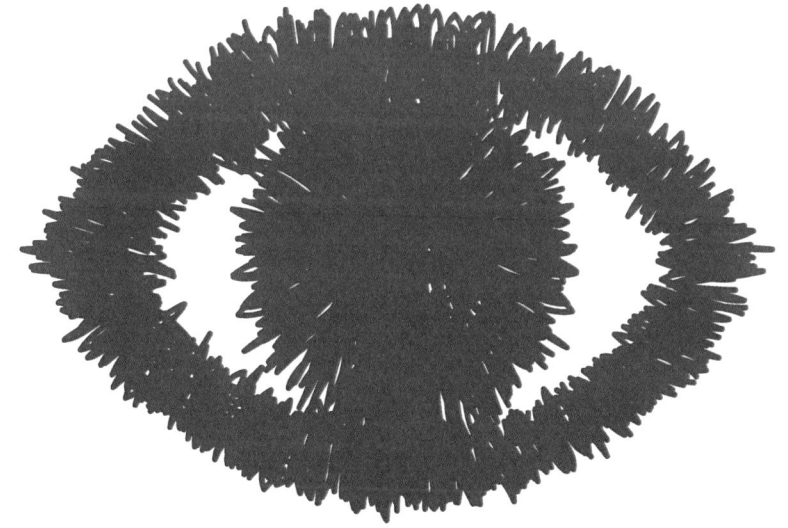

This layered umbilical cord

An elemental conduit

Has nourished a grand illusion

In the form of Separation

Now thoroughly dehydrated

Squeezed for its last ounce of deception

Effortlessly dries out

And falls off

Its purposelessness revealed

Reverse Osmosis

Reexamining the relationships

Between thought, self, and awareness

Thought identification

What does it mean?

What do I really mean?

When I say, "I am identified with thought"

For a very long minute

It seemed as if thought

Was identified with my body

But, experientially, I know

That thought is quite plainly

A continuous, conditional stream of consciousness

Reexamine from a new perspective

A different angle

I am identified with thought

What do I mean by "I"?

Until this moment

It was not entirely clear to me

And I had not realized

That my understanding was incomplete

My realization far from absolute

The "I" that was my reference point

The "I" that I thought was identified

Was itself the illusory "self"

Somehow

It had wound itself up

Did a somersault

And positively presumed the position of "I"

In order words

"Thought" presumed to realize its attachment to "thought"

How "Unreal" is that?

As I lay in bed

In the early hours of the morning

Unperturbed by the absence of sleep

Reality Emerged

Unquestionable

I. Consciousness

I am all there is

In thought

I divide and separate myself

Into seemingly diverse multitudes

To partake in a fantastic game of chaos

A frenzied but beautiful game

Of hide and seek with myself

What a riot!

Vacillating

A forgetting

That feels real while it lasts

Like temporary amnesia

It feels very complete

During its temporal duration

But without warning

A sudden whim

An unanticipated movement

Provocation

An ordinariness

A sweet fragrance

Infused with familiarity

It permeates

And re-ignites recognition

Nenia triste

Today

I sing a song

A sorrowful dirge

Lamentation of grief

Poetry for disintegration

A hymn of passage

Final rites

For the dissolution of self

In memorial of myself who is passing

A slow death of dying, it has been

Disappointment

At the absence of a welcome host

No one to applaud

None to bask in the glory

Or claim the coveted prize

For a death well executed

From the bellows of this sad dirge

A tribute to remembrance emerges

An infinite crescendo of waves

A song of life

Vanishing "self"

Phenomenal experience

Is less of a distraction

And the body

Lags only some distance behind

But I still forget

I get lost in thought

Completely captivated

By objects of experience

Caught up with life

However

The frequency of occurrence

Is exponentially less

It's duration

Is phenomenally diminished

I, Consciousness

Naturally recognize myself

Steadily, more and more

Coda

I am aware that there are no entries between early 2022 and mid-2023. It was a time of excessive mind chatter, coupled with a grave inability to articulate any of my thoughts. And "thinking" was not alone. My sense perceptions were no less impressive. There was a myriad of experiences. Some experiences were heavenly and magical. Others not so much. Still others were cause for concern so much so that if I could have, I would have returned to prior to November 11, 2019.

Nevertheless, I do recall that, disinterest and a severe lack of energy was a major theme during that sixteen-month period.

Although my mind, in an effort to take credit, was very much pre-occupied with distinguishing or defining what I was or was not, I had no interest whatsoever in almost everything. In the few areas that still managed to capture my fleeting interest, such as playing the piano, music composition, or learning a new language, I had no motivation and no energy to engage at all. Even listening to music became a bore and household chores were most definitely a serious hassle. So, outside of the rare and momentous occasion that I completed a task, I reserved the little energy I could muster for getting to work and back. At least I could feed myself and pay my bills.

In order words, my natural inclination during that time was to sit and be still in meditation and solitary reflection. But my conditioned tendencies constantly pulled me towards action. I had to do something; achieve something. My mind was consistent in its attempt to latch on and grasp unto something; anything was far more convenient and twice as comforting as the alternative—nothing. And beneath the surface, it grumbled of the disinterest. After all, who was so intent on capturing and recording these thoughts and events on paper?

In short, I struggled against the natural flow of my energies at the time, and I suffered.

Revisiting this timeline in hindsight, I was delighted to find most, if not all of it, at the very least, comical. I had not realized that love was the background of all that pain and suffering. Indescribable, really. Because now, experientially, I know that I AM, and it is profound. I also know, without a doubt, that I do not know what I AM. Equally profound. Any additions would be utter make-belief. They may be magnanimous or enchanting make-belief, but they would be elaborate stories, nonetheless.

About The Author

For over eleven years, **Afoma Mpi** was a practicing attorney primarily focused on international corporate taxation and structured finance transactions for U.S. Fortune 100 multinationals.

In 2015, she was introduced to meditation and subsequently received certification and began teaching Kundalini Yoga & Meditation. She lives in Los Angeles and holds intermittent meditation gatherings, incorporating sound baths as a holistic healing modality to facilitate and nurture personal meditation practice for wellness and to provide an opportunity for the cultivation of inner stillness; that natural state of being that clears the way for conscious choice and inspired action.

IN MEMORY OF

Margit Reverdin
and
Père Nicolas Desbeoufs

afomampi@gmail.com